Really Bad Poetry Written with a Feather PEN

Terri Ricardo

BookLeaf Publishing

India | USA | UK

Presentation by *BookLeaf Publishing*

Web: www.bookleafpub.com

E-mail: info@bookleafpub.com

ISBN: 9789360947668

First edition 2024

I would like to dedicate this book to everyone that buys this book. Because of you I can tell my Mommy that someone bought my book besides her.

ACKNOWLEDGEMENT

I would like to thank BookLeaf Publishing for this opportunity.

PREFACE

This book was born from an internet writing challenge. I thought I would get some type of pleasure proving that, even an idiot like me can get a book published.

Unfortunate Cadaver

Why am I here?
How did you suddenly appear?
Where are my clothes?
Why am I so cold?
Have you seen my family?
I'm losing my sanity

Townie

She swears like a sailor
with that Irish whisper
you will surely hear her,
She knows all about the Code of Silence
she will never tell you to avoid the violence,
Bunker Hill Day is a privilege,
you're welcome to join her
and bring your village

Warrior

3

He was afraid of the dark
he had a unique spark,
He couldn't eat unless
it was allergy free,
He had Anxiety and Depression
His baseball cards were his prized possessions,
Bipolar chose him
He refused to let it win

Generation X

Can we bring back simpler times?
When payphones and street artists collected
dimes,
Hanging out in parking lots and going
parking in secret spots,
Playing hacky sac while
reciting Jack Kerouac

Boston Green Day Riot

5

The band the stage
the weed the rage,
band plays
causes dismay,
The Hatch Shell erupts
this band is corrupt,
the music stops
fans turn on the cops,
At the end of the day only trash
and a prosthetic leg are on display

Bad Minister

He got ordained online after
drinking too much wine,
He liked to brag and kept holy water
and a collar in his bag,
He often used the free clergy
parking spots
A Saint he is not

Undertow

I feel the undertow pushing me further away
how could this be on such a sunny day.
FURTHER AWAY
Maybe if I just try to float and lay,
FURTHER AWAY
I don't want to stay
FURTHER AWAY
I hear a whistle
FURTHER AWAY
Finally help is on the way

Dream

I had a dream that made no sense until it became
a real life event,
Now I think I am psychic and need a crystal ball
to practice my trick,
I can charge you money and tell you, you're
going to meet a loving honey

SHY

9

She is shy and keeps to herself,
Truth be told, she just doesn't hear very well

Inappropriate Pacts

10

Don't tell Mom I have a fake ID
Don't shut off my life support until I'm
at least a size three

Bucket LIST

11

Instead of thinking I didn't get to do this or that,
Avoid a bucket list so in the end you won't get
pissed

Tree

We traveled to the birch tree,
we climbed it pretending to be the youthful in a
movie,
we yodeled and felt free

My Sisters Killed Gizmo

13

My sisters were mad at me, so they tied Gizmo
to a tree,
In the middle of the day with all the sun rays,
I cried when he died,
He was just a toy they said, but now he is dead

The Wake

14

After I say a prayer I'm going to sit here and
stare,
Everyone else is just waiting for beer,
Here comes the ex and awkwardness,
I can't wait to leave and go home to grieve

Pet Rock

15

Get a pet rock
It will listen and not talk,
It won't eat or have stinky feet,
It won't hog the bed or mess with your head

Ukulele Princess

Ukulele strums for fun
ukulele strums in the sun,
ukulele strums the songs right
ukulele is saying goodnight

Loud

Why does everything sound twice as loud?
It is three in the morning I just want to be
sleeping on a cloud,
Even the cat purring is annoying
why is everyone snoring
this waiting to fall asleep thing is getting boring

Junk Food

Chocolate is my favorite, it is so good yet so
bad,
When I don't have any I get sad,
The three-second rule always applies
I wish I had an endless amount of chocolate
supplies

The Real Lassie is Dead

19

It took nine dogs to play Lassie, that is lots of
leashes and ashes,
If she were still alive, she would be
approximately sixty-five

Brain

Why did you take my vision?
I had no part in that decision,
Why did you take my memory?
I can't get past one two three,
Why did you take my motor skills?
I will never be able to climb that big hill

Thank you

I want to thank you
for not flushing this book with your poo,
you are a fox, for thinking outside the box,
keep bad poetry on trend
so the joy of reading this
book never ends